CAREERS IN

PUBLIC RELATIONS

PUBLIC RELATIONS PROFESSIONALS ARE image makers. They painstakingly craft the way the public views businesses, organizations, celebrities – anyone or anything of note. If people know about it, chances are the credit goes to a public relations professional working hard behind the scenes.

PR specialists crave the spotlight for someone else. They mark success by seeing their client's name in lights. Publicists never hesitate to sing the praises about anyone or anything they represent. A PR pro cannot wait to get asked the question: So what's new?

When you are in the public relations field, if there is one person who does not know about your client, you have work to do. Public relations is a hard-charging, nonstop, take-no-prisoners business, where you get the buzz going about your client and keep it going day after day. Your goal is to set the trends, not follow them.

People who work in public relations shy away from nothing. Pushing the envelope is par for the course. You are encouraged to come up with innovative, over-the-top ways of getting the word out. The business thrives on fresh ideas, and cannot get enough of them.

Each day presents a new opportunity to get your client's brand out to the public. If those opportunities don't present themselves, you make them happen. Creative excitement is always in the air, because groundbreaking ways of communicating with the public rule the day in this field.

In public relations you take the mundane and make it exciting. You turn the ordinary into the exceptional. It's discovering those hidden gems that make the field so rewarding.

People often ask, "What will they think of next?" Whatever it is, as a public relations professional, you are the one who will let folks know about it.

A whole range of talents and skills are required to practice public relations, from crisp, imaginative writing to precise planning and superior organization. This is a job where you will be tested every day. If you like encountering the unexpected, you will definitely find it in this business, where coming up with inspired solutions to unforeseen events makes you a marquee player.

In public relations, you will never be just another employee. Your insights and advice have a major impact on the company or organization you work for, or the clients you represent. You are a pivotal cog in the wheel, right in the middle of the action.

When something goes awry, you are the one called in to fix it. When everything is going well, you are the one who gets the nod. When the time comes to take a bold step, you are the one everyone looks to for a new idea.

There is no job better suited for this information age than one that has been relied on for decades to get the word out to the masses. Whether it is referred to as public information, media relations, public affairs, corporate communications, or, as it is more commonly known, public relations, this is a career that speaks for itself and many others.

WHAT YOU CAN DO NOW

NONPROFIT ORGANIZATIONS ARE always looking for volunteers. One of the departments at a nonprofit you can volunteer to work in is public relations. Medium to large nonprofits usually have very active publicity departments. Nonprofits count on their public relations efforts to keep the public informed about all the good work the organization does in the community. That is how nonprofits get the donations and volunteers needed to keep going, and how they reach out to people who require their help and services.

Nonprofits usually hold several major events throughout the year. By helping to promote those events, you will gain excellent insight into the work that is necessary to mount a successful publicity campaign. The best part is that you can volunteer for an organization whose mission you support, so you can bolster the cause while you are learning about a career in PR. You will also have a chance to see if you like the often hectic world of public relations.

Smaller community groups also publicize events they sponsor. These organizations usually have volunteers handling their public relations, but these volunteers are often retired professional PR people who want to stay active. If you do a volunteer stint with one of these groups, it can be a valuable experience, because you will see public relations practiced on the grassroots level.

Schools are always putting on plays or doing fundraisers to help one club or another. These need to be publicized as well, so consider volunteering to handle the publicity for these events.

Whether you are trying to publicize a major event or a small one, the effort is the same. You have to figure out the best way to interest the news media in the event so you can get publicity for it. This is how many people who become PR professionals first get started in the field.

HISTORY OF THE CAREER

EVER SINCE THERE HAS BEEN SOCIAL interaction, people have recognized the need for good public relations. It was not called public relations in the 24th century BC, when Ptahhotep, the advisor to an Egyptian pharaoh, convinced the leader of the wisdom of communicating with the people regularly. But that was essentially what he was advocating.

Early on, those who understood public relations knew it could be a powerful, persuasive tool. When explorer Erik "The Red" Thorvaldson wanted to attract settlers from Iceland to an uninhabited ice- and snow-covered piece of land in the North Atlantic, he called the desolate territory "Greenland" to convey the image of a warmer climate. He led a group of settlers there in 985 AD and set up two colonies on the land's southwest coast, which is only warm enough several months a year for anything "green" to grow.

Even in the American colonies, several years before the Revolutionary War, public relations was employed to support the case for independence from Great Britain. One of the nation's founding fathers, Samuel Adams, was often singled out for his extraordinary ability to use publicity to promote the patriots' cause. However, he was not alone in this effort. Thomas Jefferson, Alexander Hamilton, Benjamin Franklin, and John Adams were among the other patriots who knew how to attract public attention with well-crafted publicity campaigns aimed at persuading colonists to break from Great Britain.

US political figures have always appreciated the importance of public relations. Shortly after taking office as President of the United States in 1829, Andrew Jackson put former journalist Amos Kendell in charge of, among other things, publicity at the White House. Kendell was the first to hold the job that would later become known as White House press secretary.

Business leaders jumped on the public relations bandwagon as well. P. T. Barnum built a circus empire by using clever publicity techniques to promote his shows in the mid- to late 1800s.

The first corporate communications department was started by businessman George Westinghouse in 1889. He used it to keep the public informed about his electric company's latest innovations. General Electric followed suit in 1897.

There is no specific date when the term "public relations" was first used, but many historians agree that the phrase was coined in the United States around the turn of the 20th century. It is known that three former newspaper reporters, George V. S. Michaelis, Thomas Marvin, and Herbert Small, started the first publicity agency in the country in 1900 in Boston. Called the Publicity Bureau, the firm represented a number of large companies, including railroads.

In 1902 another former newspaper reporter, William Wolff Smith, opened the nation's second public relations agency, this one in Washington, DC. Smith's agency was designed to use publicity to influence the decisions made by federal legislators.

Then in 1905, journalists George Parker and Ivy Lee teamed up to start a public relations firm in New York City that would set the profession on a new course. They pledged to provide information about their clients that was authentic and accurate. This would be in contrast to some publicists who commonly exaggerated the facts or covered up the truth. Lee believed that if the information he gave out about his clients was based on fact and could be proved to be truthful, it would build trust among his clients, the media, and the public.

He got the opportunity to prove his theory in 1906. Lee's firm was hired by the Pennsylvania Railroad that year, shortly after the company had a train wreck. Lee counseled his new client to invite reporters to the scene of the accident to report the facts. He also recommended that the railroad put out a press release containing the full details of what happened, covering up nothing about the mishap.

The company took Lee's advice and received favorable media coverage. The Pennsylvania Railroad quickly regained the public's confidence. Lee is called the father of public relations by many, though others give that title to Edward Bernays.

Bernays, who came to prominence in the PR business in the 1920s, believed in staging spectacular media events to get his clients publicity, such as soap-carving competitions to promote Ivory soap for his client, Procter & Gamble. Besides opening a public relations firm in 1919, he also taught public relations at New York University. He wrote *Crystallizing Public Opinion* in 1923, considered the first textbook on public relations. Throughout his career, Bernays orchestrated events for his clients that would stand out as newsworthy.

In 1927, AT&T hired Arthur W. Page, a young public relations specialist, to lead its publicity efforts. Page agreed to take the job only if he had a voice in company policy, and AT&T agreed to his terms. Page believed the policies of a company must meet with public approval. Under Page's leadership, the AT&T Publicity Department was designed "to act all the time from the public point of view, even when that seems to conflict with the operating point of view." Many of his public relations principles are still practiced today, including telling the truth, listening to the customer, managing for tomorrow, and conducting public relations as if the whole company depends on it.

As communications technology continued to grow in the United States, so did the public relations field. Television, for example, gave a big boost to the public relations business in the 1950s and 1960s, providing a new way to reach the public.

Staying in touch with their customer base became a top priority of rapidly expanding companies in the 1970s and 1980s. Corporate public relations departments met this goal by keeping the public informed about the latest products, breakthroughs, and accomplishments of these companies.

Today, in a very media-conscious world, just about every type of enterprise must have a public relations component to be successful.

WHERE YOU WILL WORK

WE ARE SURROUNDED BY PUBLIC relations. Publicists work for every industry, nonprofit, profession, and celebrity. Therefore, there is a wide range of choices when it comes to searching for a job in publicity.

Well-known public relations firms, or boutiques, as they are also called, are the prime target of those looking for work as PR specialists. At one time, big, established public relations firms were only located in large cities, but not today. They can now be found everywhere.

What these boutiques offer PR specialists is a diversity of clients. Public relations specialists work on a variety of accounts, from businesses to nonprofits – whatever types of clients the firm handles. You are usually assigned to more than one account at a time. Some public relations firms specialize in handling celebrity clients, like movie, television, and stage stars; musicians; motivational speakers; authors; or an eclectic mix of all of them.

At PR firms, the most prestigious accounts, the ones with bigger budgets, are the bailiwick of the firm's senior members. Newer hires usually deal with smaller accounts with less money to spend on a PR campaign. Though these firms usually have quite a varied range of clients, in the early stages of your career you rarely get a chance to choose what client you will be assigned. Early on, you might get saddled with a client you just don't get along with, or whose organization or profession you have no particular interest in. That shouldn't matter in the public relations industry. You must be able to work with all types of clients and put your personal preferences aside.

If you would like to become involved in publicity in a particular industry, such as real estate, pharmaceuticals, construction, entertainment, book publishing, or food, for example, you can apply for a job in corporate public relations. The corporate PR department focuses on the work of a single company in a single industry. You are an employee of that company and part of corporate America. Broadcast companies, movie studios, sports franchises, restaurant chains, resorts, cruise lines, theme parks, and retail stores are all part of corporate America, with some pretty exciting job opportunities in their PR departments.

Nonprofits are an interesting alternative for those looking for a career in public relations, but who are determined to promote something they feel passionate about. There are thousands of nonprofit organizations that support everything from education to healthcare to social and consumer issues. If you work for a nonprofit organization, you can wind up working almost anywhere – from the offices of a crusading organization trying to save the environment, find a cure for cancer, or fight for the rights of the homeless. You might work for a hospital, a religious institution, a college campus, a museum, or even a zoo.

Government agencies, from the local to the federal level, also have public relations officers on staff. These PR professionals disseminate information to the public about the agencies and the services they offer. Elected state and federal officials also hire PR specialists.

Some public relations specialists choose to found their own PR firms, starting out small and developing the business. These public relations entrepreneurs may open offices in suburban and rural areas, away from the bustling city. They offer PR services to smaller nonprofits and local businesses that do not have large budgets for publicity but still want to attract both media and public attention.

THE WORK YOU WILL DO

IN PUBLIC RELATIONS, YOU CAN change the old saying "You only get one chance to make a good first impression" to "You only get one chance to make a good *lasting* impression." The decisions you make in handling the public relations for a person, company, or organization you represent can have an impact on them, and how the public views them, for years, even decades, to come.

One of the boldest public relations decisions ever made came in October 1982. That was when Johnson & Johnson had to decide how to handle a crisis that could have crippled the company.

Seven deaths in the Chicago area were linked to one of Johnson & Johnson's most successful products – Tylenol. At the time, Tylenol had a 37 percent share of the market for pain relievers. All seven people died after taking Extra-Strength Tylenol capsules.

The suspicious deaths began in late September 1982 and continued over the course of a few days. Detectives discovered that the Extra-Strength Tylenol in question had been laced with deadly cyanide. It was determined that the product had been tampered with after it had reached store shelves in the Chicago area.

The deaths and their link to Tylenol prompted a nationwide panic. It also triggered a string of copycat crimes. Johnson & Johnson reacted quickly, putting the safety of the public ahead of its own financial well-being. That was an unprecedented move for a large corporation in crisis.

Corporate crises in the past were almost always handled by putting the company's best interest ahead of public safety, and that strategy usually backfired. Despite the fact that the tampering was not the company's fault, Johnson & Johnson took full responsibility for it.

Johnson & Johnson alerted the public nationwide, through

the news media, not to use any type of Tylenol until the full extent of the product tampering was known. They recalled about 31 million bottles of Tylenol at a cost of $100 million to the company. All advertising and production of the product were stopped. The company encouraged people who had purchased Extra-Strength Tylenol capsules, and had them in their medicine cabinet, to return them to the store where they had been purchased and get a refund.

The company made its top officials, including the chairman of the board, available to the news media. Johnson & Johnson executives also cooperated in the investigation with the FBI, the Food and Drug Administration, and Chicago area police. Even as this phase of the public relations program to handle the crisis was going on, the company was working on ways of bringing the product back to store shelves with a new tamper proof design.

In November 1982, six weeks after the crisis began, the company reintroduced Extra-Strength Tylenol to the public and started rebuilding its customer base. The product was offered with coupons and at a price reduction. It had a triple-seal, tamper proof packaging that became industry standard. By the end of 1982, Tylenol's market share for pain relievers was back up to 24 percent, well on its way to a full recovery.

How Johnson & Johnson dealt with the Tylenol case has become legendary in the public relations profession, when it comes to crisis management, or damage control. It was hailed by the media. The Washington Post wrote, "Johnson & Johnson has effectively demonstrated how a major business ought to handle a disaster."

As the missteps of celebrities, companies, and organizations are played up in the news media and the social media more than ever before, public relations specialists have to be ready to defuse these PR nightmares. Effective crisis management and damage control have to be part of every publicist's repertoire. The client's future may depend on it.

This is where you call upon your talents for creative problem solving and become invaluable to your client. Any bad press or negative public comments have to be responded to immediately. A small brush fire can spread quickly.

Crises aside, there is plenty of work public relations specialists do on a day-to-day basis. It is the job of the PR person to keep a client's name in the public eye. That starts with press releases, the heart of any public relations strategy. Press releases are the way public relations specialists keep the news media and the public aware of the latest activities and breaking news involving a client.

At one time a press release was only shared with the news media. Today, besides going to news outlets, press releases are often posted directly on the web, allowing publicists to get the message out directly to the target audience.

Press releases have to be well written and newsworthy. Even though publicists are playing to a target audience, they always want to go beyond that group to garner more interest for their client and expand the client's customer base.

The intent of the press release is to get news coverage. News stories about a person, company, or organization are much different than advertising. Advertisements are paid for by a client. Advertisers can say whatever they want in an ad. They have complete editorial control over an ad and decide where and when it runs. It takes much more work for a public relations specialist to get a story covered by the news media. However, it is well worth the effort. The public knows the difference between a news article and an advertisement. A news story has much more credibility with the public than a paid ad.

The publicist has to approach the news media with a solid news angle on a story and back it up with facts. The story has to pique the interest of an editor and have an impact on the lives of a sizable number of people. Good public relations specialists must know the difference between news and fluff. They have to make sure every press release has substance. The worst thing a PR specialist can do is waste a news editor's time with a non-story. Notable news organizations – like large newspapers and magazines, and network TV, cable TV, and radio stations – do not run puff pieces.

Even if you have a good story, with a wide appeal, the competition is fierce for newspaper or magazine space or air time on television, cable television, or radio. You have to study the news media thoroughly to figure out the kind of stories they like and lean toward covering.

PR professionals never stop cultivating their media contacts. They have contacts at all levels of the media, from local to national, weekly newspapers to network television stations, and bloggers covering the field their client specializes in.

Reporters have to be able to trust the public relations specialists they call on for information. So, as a PR person, you have to be up front with the media, while still representing the best interests of your client. This is a fine line, but one that has to be mastered to gain respect in the field and be seen as an honest, credible source of information.

Your reputation is important because the public relations specialist is often seen as the face of the company. To be effective, public relations specialists have to be up on the latest trends and know what the public is interested in. Those are the types of stories that attract the news media.

It is not good enough to just email a press release to the news media. Journalists get thousands of press releases. You have to add a personal touch to be successful. The best public relations professionals know they have to follow up, contact media outlets by phone or in person, and talk up the story.

Public relations is a two-way street. Besides sending out press releases and expecting the news media to respond, PR specialists have to respond to the news media. When contacted by reporters, publicists must be able to answer the media's questions or get the answers quickly. They have to be able to set up interviews with their clients and make sure the client is properly prepared to talk to the media.

The public relations expert knows how to seize an opportunity. All-news cable TV networks have an unending need for experts to talk about a variety of topics as these issues make headlines. This is free air time and a good way to get your clients publicity if they have expertise in a particular area, such as security, healthcare, consumer issues, or legal matters. As soon as a story breaks, you have to reach out to your media contacts with a statement from your client, as well as a reminder of that person's qualifications and proficiency in the field as it relates to the story.

A PR campaign can last a week, a month, a year, or longer. These campaigns are well-planned and are usually devised to keep a client's name in the public eye on a continuous basis. The groundwork has to be carefully laid. The goal of these efforts is for the public to see the client's name everywhere they turn, and view it in a positive way. In the long run, the ultimate objective of a national PR program is usually to make the client's brand part of American culture, like McDonald's or Walt Disney or the Red Cross. It's a lofty goal and few reach it, but even a partial success can change the fortunes of a small, unknown company or organization.

As the public relations campaign moves along, skilled publicity specialists need to hold onto the gains already made, while enhancing the program. Well-placed news stories have to appear in both local and national media. The PR professional carefully shapes the client's image, not only touting what the client does but how the client fits into and helps out in the community. No solid public relations program comes without a corporate responsibility component, showing the client giving back.

What makes the job of public relations specialists so challenging is that they have to keep a client's lines of communication open between a wide variety of groups, including consumers, stockholders, the public in general, and employees. Internal communications – staying in touch with employees – are important. A successful external PR program is based on having all the employees onboard and keeping them informed about everything the company is doing. It also helps to have a way for employees to communicate their ideas and concerns about the company.

Both the public and employees want to feel that their voices are being heard. It is up to PR specialists to give these groups the opportunity to offer some input and then give them feedback, through various communications tools, like websites, social media, blogs, newsletters, and the like.

New technology has given companies, organizations, professionals, and celebrities the ability to put out their own stories, publish their own content 24/7, and control some of the news being disseminated about them. The people working behind the scenes, making sure the message being communicated is timely, relevant, pertinent, and updated on a regular basis, are public relations professionals.

Speechwriting, and arranging for speaking engagements, also fall under your purview. Public relations professionals decide where it would be advantageous for a client to be seen. Thousands of events take place throughout the country every week. Your client's presence at a particular event that coincides with what your client does or a cause the company, organization, or individual supports can reinforce all your efforts to build strong brand recognition. It also helps to foster goodwill and reaffirm that good lasting impression you have worked so hard to put in place.

STORIES FROM THE WORLD OF PUBLIC RELATIONS

I Am in Corporate Public Relations

"I think corporate public relations today is about creating the right image for your company. I believe how people perceive your company boosts the bottom line. You can work for the biggest company in the world, but if that company takes the time to help in local communities, people view that company as more than just a moneymaking machine.

While stockholders are primarily interested in profits, I think that is very shortsighted. I guess I am old school. I feel if the local grocery store supports the high school band, townspeople take note of that, and people naturally gravitate to that store, feeling it is part of the community.

Corporations can do the same thing. Corporate responsibility is an important part of our image. As corporate PR people, we have to publicize that image, not just to the public but internally as well. Our employees have to know what our mission is, what we stand for, the causes we support.

Every one of our employees comes in contact with members of the public, and they can talk up the human side of the company just as much as a press release to the news media. Every employee needs to know that it is truly our mission to satisfy every customer – not just talk about it, but really do it, and back it up with actions.

With a national company, issues come up every day. Reporters from different parts of the country have questions and raise issues. We have to get back to them in a timely fashion with truthful answers to their questions. It can be questions about product safety, product recalls, product side effects, product distribution, environmental concerns, corporate giving, a press release you sent out, or an issue you have never been asked about before. You have to be ready for anything, and every media query has to be answered professionally and thoughtfully.

I think the most valuable piece of advice I can give anyone is that when you start out in corporate public relations, you should really take the time to get to know the company you are working for, inside and out. If it's a manufacturing concern, watch the process. If it's service-oriented, go out on some calls. Know all the products, know all the company divisions, see how complaints are handled. If the employees represent the company at community events, go with them on occasion. I believe that when you are in corporate public relations, you have to know the company better than anyone else in the building."

I Am the Director of Public Relations at a Nonprofit Organization

"I started out in corporate public relations, but my heart was always in nonprofits. I think nonprofits face an enormous task when it comes to getting their message out. There are a limited number of news outlets, and they are usually drawn to the bigger nonprofits, perhaps ones that they are already familiar with and even support.

The field is very competitive when it comes to getting mainstream news coverage, and that's what makes a public relations job at a nonprofit so challenging. Getting news coverage for all the good work a nonprofit does is vital. It leads to recognition for your organization, which often translates into volunteers and donations.

There are many worthwhile causes out there, and they all deserve to get their fair share of publicity, but that's not how it works. You have to push hard to get your nonprofit noticed by the news media. You must be creative. You have to find an unusual angle that makes what your nonprofit is doing unique.

Consider this kind of story: A child gets every player on his Little League baseball team to donate a dollar to your organization every time the team wins. That may not bring in a lot of money, but it can result in great publicity. It's a feel-good story that shows kids doing something good, caring about others, and learning about life, and it inspires others to come forward and help out as well. It can really jump-start a fundraising effort.

Seizing opportunities is an important part of the job. Many of the social ills that nonprofits address, like hunger, homelessness, illness, and poverty, make it into the headlines all the time. When they do, as the PR person for a nonprofit that addresses one of these issues, you have to let the news media know what you are doing about the problem and the help your organization provides.

I think modern technology has helped nonprofits. Websites give us a forum to get news about our organization out to the public, and in an economical way. No expensive mailings are required, and we can always draw new people to our website, 24 hours a day, where they can find out about us and what we do.

Social media and email lists let us stay in contact with our volunteers, donors, and the people we serve. Remaining on people's radar throughout the year is really half the battle. You don't want time to lag between contacts and give supporters an opportunity to get interested in a new cause or another organization. Most people have a short attention span, and you can easily lose them. Social media help us retain members, donors, and volunteers because it is easy to stay in contact with them and for them to stay in contact with us."

I Run a Small Public Relations Firm

"I think there is a big demand for small public relations firms. We really fill a niche. Large PR firms require that clients have big PR budgets or they won't take them on. Those budgets may range from $250,000 to a million dollars or more annually. Many businesses and nonprofits don't have that kind of money. That's where small PR firms come in.

Some of our clients can spend only a few thousand dollars to promote one event, but we can get them media coverage for that event. Many of these events are newsworthy, but would otherwise go by unnoticed because these businesses or organizations don't have the expertise to conduct a publicity campaign. Other clients we work with have bigger budgets, ranging from $20,000 to $50,000 or more annually, but even those budgets are way under what a bigger firm would consider working with.

Many clients are simply looking for local or regional coverage. Among our clients are restaurants, local chapters of nonprofit organizations, small businesses that service several towns, regional cultural events and theaters, and sports venues like ice skating rinks, miniature golf courses, and exercise and tennis clubs. They all have stories to tell and it's our job to get those stories out to the public.

What's most important is being able to identify a good story. What would be of interest to the local community? Chances are your clients have those stories. You just have to find them and get them out to the public. Writing an interesting, informative press release with all the facts is vital. I think what sets one press release apart from all the others that come into a media outlet is how well you present the material and how fast you get to the point.

Become familiar with the media outlets you are contacting and the types of stories they like to use. Even more important, try to make contacts at these places. I still believe in the personal touch, contacting these people by phone or going down to their office and handing them a press release.

Follow-up is very important in the public relations business. Contact the reporters and editors. Sometimes you have to give your story ideas a push, go the extra mile, show the media how much you believe in what you are promoting.

There really is no small public relations job. For the people you are representing, the work you are doing is very important. It can be a first step toward getting them some recognition and opening some doors. So you have to treat each business or nonprofit like a million-dollar client."

PERSONAL QUALIFICATIONS

PUBLIC RELATIONS SPECIALISTS ARE image makers, and that means they have to project a strong public persona themselves. People working in the field must be confident, outgoing, enthusiastic, and upbeat.

This is not a job for the timid. PR pros always have to display a "can do" attitude. Leadership abilities are vital in this job, since you tackle a variety of issues that come up from day to day.

Thinking on your feet is essential. You have to recognize an opportunity to grab the headlines and seize the moment. There are rarely second chances.

PR professionals usually work as part of a team – with other publicists, ad agencies, photographers, graphic designers, web designers, and with other departments in a company. Working well with others is a critical attribute in the field of public relations.

Building a strong, genuine rapport with the news media is necessary. That is probably the toughest part of the job, and it is a talent that not everyone can master. While you are always trying to present your client in the most positive light possible, you also have to be truthful with the media to cultivate a trusting working relationship. Your credibility can never be in question. That means walking a very fine line between protecting the interests of your client and providing the news media with the facts needed to do an accurate story.

Public relations specialists are experts at turning a run-of-the-mill story into something timely and extraordinary. That's where creativity comes into play. The ideas PR pros come up with have to be inspired and imaginative all the time. They have to find the new angle or add a different twist.

Patience, especially in public, helps a PR campaign run smoothly. No matter how much anxiety you are feeling, you have to guide your project with a steady hand.

Public relations specialists are decision makers. They know how to solve problems and do it often with ease. Good organization and planning skills will help you succeed.

Foremost are good communications skills, and that includes proficiency in both spoken and written communications. The media appreciates well-written press releases, straightforward and uncomplicated. Clearly written releases make the job of reporters and assignment editors easier.

Being a good listener cannot be underestimated. You have to understand what the person or organization you are representing wants to get across to the public. While you are using your own words and ideas to structure the campaign, the client has to be happy with how you are projecting the image.

ATTRACTIVE FEATURES

PR PROFESSIONALS DERIVE SATISFACTION from seeing a well-coordinated public relations campaign come off exactly as planned. It can be exhilarating for all involved and a career maker for some, depending on the scope of the campaign. It is pleasing to see all their hard work culminate in a great success – the hours of research, groundwork, and preparation paying off.

Capitalizing on that achievement – taking the campaign to the next level – only burnishes the accomplishment. Imagine what it is like to have people everywhere talking about something you have been promoting. You are having a positive impact on people's lives.

Public relations lets you put your ideas into action. Publicists have a chance to push the envelope, using bold, fresh, innovative, even unorthodox approaches to get their clients publicity. It is a job that encourages people to break the mold.

This is an exciting field, full of action – some days nonstop. If you like to stay busy, you will not be disappointed. As soon as one project is completed, you will be on to another, that is if you are not already working on several projects at once. Public relations rarely gets boring and usually no two days are alike. This is not the field for people who like to remain sedentary. You will constantly be on the move. Something always requires your attention.

In the PR work environment, you have a great deal of freedom and independence. Once you are handed the ball, you are expected to run with it. For those who like to lead a project from beginning to end, this is a dream job. As a public relations professional, you get the chance to take someone or something that is a complete unknown and bring it into the mainstream, make it a household name.

You will be surrounded by creative people who think outside the box and are dedicated to making the impossible happen. Events staged by public relations specialists are often glamorous, like movie previews, book and product launches, award ceremonies, art gallery and museum exhibit openings, parades, competitions, fundraising kickoffs, and a variety of social functions.

PR pros are an integral part of any company or organization. Professionals, politicians, and celebrities have publicists working for them. Your input on important issues is sought and valued.

PR specialists are often brought in to save the day, to turn a catastrophe around and right the ship. In that role, these PR pros receive all the respect that goes along with that monumental task. They are viewed as masters of public opinion, working their magic to polish a tarnished image and bring a reputation back from the brink of disaster.

UNATTRACTIVE ASPECTS

WITH ALL THE EXCITEMENT THAT surrounds a career in public relations comes a great deal of pressure, and it all falls directly on you. Public relations is about results, and those results are expected every day.

Your schedule is usually hectic. You have to handle stress, anxiety, and the demands of an extremely heavy workload. Deadlines are a regular part of this job and usually have to be met on a daily basis. That can be hard to get used to.

This is not a nine-to-five job. Unpaid overtime is par for the course, as is working nights and weekends. The field requires a deep-rooted commitment that can interfere with other personal goals.

You have to come up with ideas quickly and can never run dry. When a PR team gets together, ideas have to flow freely and plans for a publicity campaign must start taking shape as soon as possible.

This is a job that requires thick skin. Some clients are simply unreceptive to promising ideas and favor unworkable approaches. You will encounter a great deal of rejection in the PR business, and you must get used to that and shrug it off. No one in the PR business has a 100 percent success rate. Some publicity campaigns simply do not work, regardless of the research and planning that go into them. You cannot take rejection personally.

What you think is a great idea for a publicity campaign may be dismissed by your client out of hand. A pitch you give to several reporters that you think is a perfect fit for their media outlets may fall on deaf ears. Being able to regroup, present new ideas, and make another pitch must seem natural to you.

In the PR field you always work behind the scenes and usually get little credit for your accomplishments. When you first start out in the publicity field, others may take credit for your work. Office politics can be intense, so the business requires you to have an assertive personality.

The world of public relations is very competitive, both from within the business and externally, as you try to get the media to pay attention to the client you are representing.

Today the tools of the PR trade are constantly evolving. New ways to communicate emerge all the time, with groundbreaking and novel social media platforms. What is popular now may be outdated next week. It takes time to learn how to use these innovative tools and measure their success.

EDUCATION AND TRAINING

MOST PEOPLE PLANNING TO GO INTO the PR field set their sights on getting a college degree in public relations. Others may get a degree in communications, marketing, advertising, or journalism. Some people manage to break into the field with excellent writing skills and a bachelor's degree in English.

Those looking to hire public relations professionals lean toward people with majors or degrees in public relations, primarily because most of the colleges with these programs require students to complete an internship to get their degree.

Traditionally, public relations specialists came from the ranks of journalists, since the skills for journalism and public relations are so closely related. Journalism is still a good entrée into the public relations field. However, it is not uncommon these days to see people bypass the journalism degree, along with the stint at a news organization, in favor of getting a bachelor's degree in public relations and going directly into a PR job.

St. John's University's College of Professional Studies in New York City is addressing the needs of students looking to enter the PR field with its Bachelor of Science degree in public relations. The program is renowned for keeping pace with the rapidly changing dynamics in the world of public relations and the ever-expanding methods of communicating with the public.

It accomplishes this by integrating information about the latest communications technologies and approaches to PR. Emphasized are the ability to create messages for a variety of audiences, techniques used to gain insight into a customer base, and the importance of critical thinking and analysis. The program focuses on corporate communications, marketing communications, and brand communications.

The University of Texas at Austin was one of the first colleges to offer a bachelor's degree in public relations. Offered through the Stan Richards School of Advertising & Public Relations, the PR program includes courses such as Writing for Public Relations, Fundamentals of Public Relations, Public Relations Techniques, Strategies in Public Relations, and Integrated Communications Management. An internship in public relations is also required.

Chicago is the perfect backdrop for Loyola University's advertising/public relations program, which results in a bachelor's degree from the institution's School of Communication. Because of the school's location in one of the nation's major advertising and public relations markets, working professionals visit the school regularly to take part in panel discussions, give lectures, and talk to students on a one-on-one basis about the world of public relations and advertising. Students also have a wide range of internships to choose from, in public relations agencies, corporations, and nonprofits.

Students who major in public relations at the University Of South Carolina (USC) in Columbia can participate in the Carolina Agency. The agency is a student-run public relations and advertising firm at the university. At the agency, students work with real clients, developing award-winning PR campaigns.

PR Management, Public Relations Campaigns, Graphic Design, and Public Relations Writing are among the courses students take at the University of South Carolina to fulfill the school's requirements for a Bachelor of Arts degree in journalism and mass communications with a major in public relations. USC also helps students find internships and mentors in public relations.

When majoring in public relations at Ferris University in Big Rapids, Michigan, students learn both to write a press release and to read a spreadsheet. That is because the Public Relations Department is in the university's School of Business and there is a creative as well as a business angle. Principles of Public Relations, Public Relations Law and Ethics, Marketing Research, and Public Relations Tactics are some of the courses. Graduates majoring in public relations at Ferris University have an excellent track record in finding jobs in all areas of public relations.

Seton Hall University in South Orange, New Jersey offers a Bachelor of Arts degree in journalism and public relations. Students who choose the public relations track prepare to enter the world of corporate communications, PR for nonprofit organizations, and integrated marketing communications, among other related jobs. They also learn about the news media and working with the 24-hour news cycle.

The University of Southern California, Los Angeles has both undergraduate and graduate programs in public relations at its Annenberg School for Communications and Journalism. The university's graduates are heavily recruited by some of the nation's top corporations and nonprofits.

Other colleges and universities with noteworthy programs in public relations include Florida Southern College in Lakeland, Florida; Chapman University in Orange, California; Kent State University in Kent, Ohio; Marquette University in Milwaukee; the University of Alabama in Tuscaloosa; Illinois State University in Normal, Illinois; and Hawaii Pacific University in Honolulu.

EARNINGS

SALARIES IN PUBLIC RELATIONS VARY greatly, depending on where you work. Large public relations firms lead the way when it comes to the biggest paychecks for public relations executives. These executives can earn $250,000 or more a year, depending on the client base.

Public relations specialists who are go-getters, with 10-plus years of experience but not on the executive level, can achieve earnings in the $150,000 range from an upper-crust PR firm. Salaries are not quite so high in smaller firms, however, it all comes down to the client roster. There are usually incentives for employees who sign up new clients.

Corporations are the next highest earnings sector. PR specialists can enter corporate work in the $40,000 to $50,000 salary range, even for a first job. The prospects for advancement for hard workers in the corporate world are excellent. Public relations directors at major corporations have yearly incomes of $175,000 or more. Even at smaller companies, public relations managers or directors can bring home earnings that hover around the $100,000 mark.

Large nationwide nonprofits with big budgets and strong fundraising capabilities can offer competitive salaries that match the corporate world. The earnings drop off for public relations executives at smaller nonprofits with tighter budgets. The range is between $75,000 and $100,000 for PR directors. Entry-level public relations jobs at nonprofits usually start low, in the $35,000 to $40,000 range, based on the size of the organization.

OPPORTUNITIES

GOOD PUBLIC RELATIONS PROFESSIONALS are more sought after now than ever before. PR is a growing field, because there are so many new ways of communicating being introduced all the time.

Experts predict there will be almost a 25 percent increase in jobs throughout the country over the next decade. The upswing is attributed in part to new companies starting up – especially in technology – which are hiring PR people to promote them. In addition, existing companies are expanding their publicity efforts, recognizing the increasing importance of staying in touch with their customer base through the myriad of online communications tools. Blogging and Facebook pages are valuable new tools for reaching out to a company's customer base, but someone has to create them, and that offers opportunities for public relations specialists.

There was once a concern in the PR industry that the decline in print publications, like newspapers and magazines, spelled doom for public relations. Fewer publications would mean fewer places to get publicity for clients. The opposite has proved true. There has been huge growth in other areas, including digital media, social media, and cable television. While PR pros are focusing on the new technology, they cannot lose sight of the traditional media, either, and must make sure their clients have a presence there as well.

All the new communications technology has caused companies, nonprofits, and even government agencies that never dabbled in public relations to become interested in developing a traditional media campaign and an online presence. Having your brand in the public eye is considered a necessity today. That means more jobs for public relations professionals. With all the new companies, products, technologies, nonprofits, and celebrities looking to get their brands out to the public comes more competition for people's attention. Devising imaginative ways to grab the public's interest is driving the PR market.

Some PR firms are finding niche markets helping companies become more consumer-friendly. Things are changing so rapidly in the technology field that people are having trouble keeping up with all the latest developments. At times, they need some of it explained to them in layman's terms. This has opened up an entire new sector in public relations for specialists who understand technology and can explain it to the rest of us.

These tech PR experts work with companies that develop new technology. They disseminate press releases about how this technology impacts everyday life and can benefit everybody. It is hard to get people to buy into a new technology if they do not understand how it works or why they need it. Public relations keeps people in the loop.

GETTING STARTED

ONCE YOU HAVE MADE THE DECISION to go into public relations, the next important step is to develop a plan to reach your career goal. There are so many paths you can follow – corporate, agency, government, nonprofit – and each one is different and may not be interesting, satisfying, or fulfilling to everybody.

PR is known for having a high turnover rate, primarily because people go into it without careful planning. You have to be motivated, you have to be excited, you have to believe in what you are promoting, and you have to be determined to spread the word about it.

It's not about getting that first job, it's about getting the right first job. If you accept a job in corporate public relations when you really want to work in the nonprofit sector, that can be a disaster, souring you on the entire profession. So plan carefully. Look into the various aspects of the field, and see what you like and dislike about each one.

There are plenty of internships in public relations. It is a good idea to take on several of them in different aspects of the business throughout college to gain experience in the field and see which appeals to you most.

More likely than not, you will find you are better suited within one facet of the field. Even in corporate public relations, for example, you may discover that you would much rather work with fashion than sports, with electronics than food. PR jobs in all these areas abound. You just have to do your homework.

Part of PR is research and this can be your first assignment. When you go on job interviews, know as much as possible about the company or organization you are approaching. Not only can you talk intelligently about the job you are expected to do, but it shows that you arrive prepared and ready to take on responsibility. Part of public relations is thinking ahead. When you enter a job interview knowledgeable about the company or organization, what they do and stand for, it shows you are ready to hit the ground running.

After the interview, send an email thank you, followed by a handwritten or typed note with a slightly different message, to the people you met with, expressing your appreciation for the time they spent with you. Do not forget to mention why you feel you are the right person for the job. This is public relations, so promote yourself!

It is never a bad idea for people going into public relations to spend some time on the other side, that is, in a newsroom. You can keep up your writing skills while learning what reporters and editors are looking for in stories and press releases. Many PR people start out as journalists. The insights you will gain as a reporter are extremely valuable, and even more important are the contacts and friendships you make in the news business. Those relationships can last and be beneficial for your entire career.

ASSOCIATIONS

■ **Public Relations Society of America (PRSA)**
http://www.prsa.org

■ **Council of Public Relations Firms (also known as PR Council)**
http://www.prfirms.org

■ **Public Relations Student Society of America (PRSSA)**
http://prssa.prsa.org

■ **Washington Women in Public Relations (WWPR)**
http://wwpr.org

■ **National Black Public Relations Society (NBPRS)**
http://www.nbprs.org

■ **Hispanic Public Relations Association (HPRA)**
http://www.hpra-usa.org

PERIODICALS

■ **PR Week**

■ **PR News**

■ **The Public Relations Strategist**

- Public Relations Journal
- Public Relations Review
- Public Relations Tactics
- O'Dwyer's Newsletter
- O'Dwyer's Monthly Magazine

WEBSITES

- Ragan's PR Daily
  http://www.prdaily.com/Main/Home.aspx

- O'Dwyer's PR Daily
  http://www.odwyerpr.com

- Publicity Club of New England
  http://www.pubclub.org

- Publicity Club of New York (PCNY)
  http://www.publicityclub.org

- Publicity Club of Chicago (PCC)
  http://publicity.org

- New York Women in Communications Inc.
  (NYWICI)
  http://www.nywici.org

- Entertainment Publicists Professional Society
  (EPPS)
  http://www.eppsonline.org/home/index.php/home

- National Association of Government
  Communicators (NAGC)
  http://www.nagconline.org

■ **Institute for Public Relations (IPR)**
http://www.instituteforpr.org

■ **Florida PR Association (FPRA)**
http://www.fpra.org

■ **Philadelphia Public Relations Association (PPRA)**
http://ppra.net

■ **International Public Relations Association (IPRA)**
http://www.ipra.org

■ **International Association of Business Communicators (IABC)**
http://www.iabc.com